D0436864

the Witches' Spell Book

by CERRIDWEN GREENLEAF

RUNNING PRESS

PHILADELPHIA · LONDON

A Running Press® Miniature Edition™
© 2013 by Running Press
All rights reserved under the Pan-American and International
Copyright Conventions
Printed in China

9 8 7
Digit on the right indicates the number of this printing

Library of Congress Control Number: 2013933268

ISBN 978-0-7624-5081-7

Running Press Book Publishers
A Member of the Perseus Books Group
2300 Chestnut Street
Philadelphia, PA 19103-4371

Visit us on the web!
www.runningpress.com

a CHARMED LIFE

For centuries, witches have known that luck is neither random nor mysterious. Thanks to the wise women in my family who shared their "trade secrets" openly, I learned very early in life that my fate was mine to guide, and that I could manifest my will through the tools of magic. I have never used witchcraft specifically to get money, but I have used it to find a good home, attract job opportunities, and help others. People have always marveled at what they perceive as my "good luck," or suggested that I have a fleet of guardian angels behind my every move. But luck and angels have nothing to do with it.

As soon as you approach your magic consciously, you will see that you have the power to choose abundance. And when you increase your material prosperity, you reduce the need to worry about such worldly matters. Then you can move on to achieving true prosperity: pursuing your pleasures, spending time with family and friends, and enjoying your life.

Magic and spellwork is about expansion—expanding your horizons, enriching your mind and spirit, and celebrating the real riches of health and happiness. Every witch walks her spiritual path with practical feet and is aware of the fiercely competitive world in which we live. With life's increasingly frantic pace, the search for serenity is now more important than ever.

Herein lie the keys to rising above the fray and embracing a life of abundance and joy. Every day is an opportunity for growth in every aspect of your life, and the level of success is entirely up to you. Think of the following spells and charms as pagan prescriptions for the twenty-first century, guaranteed to banish stress, ease tension, and add comfort, joy, and magic to your daily life. Blessed be!

EVERYDAY SACRED: *a* RITUAL GUIDE TO THE DAYS OF THE WEEK

Each day of the week has specific correspondences and meanings. Here is an at-a-glance guide to the days of the week, gleaned from the mythologies of centuries put to practice for different types of ritual. I do a money-enhancing ritual every Thursday, or "Thor's Day," which is the day for prosperity. Perhaps you want new love in your life; if so, try a "Freya's Day" ritual on a Friday night.

Sunday is the day for healing and vitality, as well as creativity and new hope. The colors for this day are gold, orange, and yellow, and the sacred stones for this day are also in those colors, amber, citrine, carnelian, and topaz. Sunday's herbs and incense are cloves, cedar, chamomile, frankincense, amber, sunflower, and heliotrope.

Monday, or "Moon Day," is a dreamy day for intuition, beauty, women's rituals, and your home. The colors are shiny silvers, pearl, pale rose, white, and lavender, reflective like the moon. The gems and stones are similarly shaded moonstone, pearl, quartz crystal, fluorite, and aquamarine. The herbs and incense are night blooming jasmine, myrtle, moonwort, vervain, white rose, poppy, and camphor.

Tuesday is the day for action. "Mars's Day" is the time for high energy in your career, for physical activity, for aggression in meetings, and for strong sensuality. Red is the day's color, and the corresponding gems and crystals are ruby, garnet, carnelian, bloodstone, and pink tourmaline. Incense and herbs for Mars's

Day are red roses, pine, carnation, nettle, patchouli, pepper, and garlic.

Wednesday, or "Odin's Day," is when the planets of communication, Mercury and Chiron, rule. This is the optimum time for writing, public speaking, intellectual pursuits, memory, and all other forms of communication. Colors for this day are light blue, gray, green, orange, and yellow. The crystals are sodalite, moss agate, opal, and aventurine. The herbs and incense are cinnamon, periwinkle, dill, sweet pea, cinquefoil, and ferns.

Thursday is the day for business, politics, legalities, bargaining, good fortune, and material and fiscal wealth. The colors are blue, purple, and turquoise. As you might suspect, the crystals are turquoise, sapphire, amethyst, and lapis lazuli, so favored by the Egyptians. The herbs and incense for the day are saffron, cedar, nutmeg, pine, oak, and cinnamon.

Friday is ruled by Freya, the Nordic Venus, goddess of love. Friday is all about beauty, love, sex, fertility, friendships and partnerships, the arts, harmony and music, and bringing the new into your life. Pale green and deep green, robin's-egg blue, pink, and violet are the colors, and the crystals are emerald, pink tourmaline, rose quartz, as well as jade, malachite, and peridot. The herbs and incense for Fridays are apple, lily, birch, pink rose, verbena, ivy, rose, and sage.

Saturday is a time for protection, discipline, duty, binding, family, manifestation, and completion. Saturday's crystals are amethyst, smoky quartz, jet, black onyx, obsidian, and darkest garnet. The incense, plants, and herbs for this day are ivy, oak, rue, moss, myrrh, deadly nightshade, mandrake, hemlock, and wolfsbane. (Many Saturn herbs are toxic; please exercise caution when using them.)

LIGHTING *the* ETERNAL FLAME

*W*hen the first narrow crescent of the waxing moon appears in the twilight sky, place a green candle beside a white lily or freesia. White flowers have the most intense aromas. Anoint the candle with tuberose or rose oil. Take a handful of seeds such as sunflower, wal-

nuts, or pistachios, still in their shells,
and place them in front of the candle.

Close your eyes and recite aloud:

Under the newest of moons,
In Eden fair, I walk through flowers
In the garden of my desires,
I light the flame of my mind,
I plant the seeds of things to come.

SANCTUARY *and* SERENITY MAGICAL POTPOURRI

*P*otpourri was a medieval product revived by the Victorians, who used the symbolic meanings and powers of flowers. Grow flowers in your kitchen garden or buy cut flowers. Dry them; then place them in a pretty container. Choose flowers that connect with your astrological sign and personal energy.

Flower essences mixed with 30 millimeters distilled water can also be used as the following remedies:

Addiction: *skullcap, agrimony*

Anger: *nettle, blue flag, chamomile*

Anxiety: *garlic, rosemary, aspen, periwinkle, lemon balm, white chestnut, gentian*

Bereavement: *honeysuckle*

Depression: *borage, sunflower, larch, chamomile, geranium, yerba santa, black cohosh, lavender, mustard*

Exhaustion: *aloe, yarrow, olive, sweet chestnut*

Fear: *poppy, mallow, ginger, peony, water lily, basil, datura*

Heartbreak: *heartsease, hawthorn, borage*

Lethargy: *aloe, thyme, peppermint*

Stress: *dill, echinacea, thyme, mistletoe, lemon balm*

Spiritual blocks: *oak, ginseng, lady's slipper*

BLESSED BALM SPELL

Simmer this mixture whenever you feel the need to infuse your home and heart with the energies of protection. This will safeguard you and your loved ones from outside influences that could be negative or disruptive. Set your intention and gather together the following herbs:

1 cup rosemary
1 teaspoon dill weed
4 bay laurel leaves
1 cup cedar
1 tablespoon basil
1 teaspoon juniper berries
1 cup sage

Mix your herbs together by hand.
While you are doing this, close your
eyes and visualize your home as a
sacred place protected by a boundary

of glowing white light. Add the herbs to a pan filled with simmering water.

When the aromatic steam rises, intone:

By my own hand, I have made this balm;

This divine essence contains my calm.

By my own will, I make this charm;

This precious potpourri protects all
  from harm.
With harm to none and health to all,
Blessed be!

NEW MOON FLOWER POWER

This flower-infused pot-pourri is wonderful for clearing the way for the new in your life and planting "seeds" for new moon beginnings. You can also create a wreath with garlic bulbs for self-protection and insurance that your newly laid plans won't go awry.

Flower ingredients:
Rose · Snapdragon · Marigold
Carnation · Cyclamen

Place the flowers in a bowl and then sprinkle them with a few drops of geranium, clove, and cinnamon oil. Place the mixture on the south point of your altar for the duration of a full lunar cycle, from new moon to new moon.

CRYSTAL CLEAR

Whenever you acquire a new crystal, you need to cleanse it.

Gather these elemental energies:

A candle for fire

A cup of water

Incense for air

A bowl of salt

Pass your crystal through the scented
smoke of the incense and say:

Inspired with the breath of air

Pass the crystal swiftly through the
flame of the candle and say:

Burnished by fire

Sprinkle the crystal with
water and say:

Purified by water

Dip the crystal into the bowl
of salt and say:

Empowered by the earth

Hold the crystal before you with
both hands and imagine an
enveloping, warm white light
purifying the tool. Now say:

Steeped in spirit and bright with light

Place the cleansed crystal
upon your altar and say:

*By craft made and by craft charged
and changed, this crystal I will use for
the purpose of good in this world and
in the realm of the gods and goddesses.
I hereby consecrate this crystal.*

PROSPERITY ALTAR: USING the LAWS of ATTRACTION

You can increase your prosperity by remembering one of the most basic principles of prosperity: *By giving, so shall you receive.* To create a prosperity altar, consecrate the area with sea salt. Cover a low table with green and gold altar cloths or scarves and place matching candles on it. Each day, "recharge" your altar with an altar gift such as flowers, jade or other green crystals, golden flowers, scented amber resin, and coin-shaped pebbles.

BY JOVE!
a SPELL FOR WEALTH

On any Thursday or new moon, light your altar candle at midnight and burn frank-incense and myrrh incense. Make an offering of a golden fruit, such as apples or peaches, to Jupiter, and anoint your third eye with a corresponding essential oil, such as myrrh, frankincense, apple, or peach.

Pray aloud:
This offering I make as my blessing to all.
Greatest of gods, Lord Jove of the sky.
From you, all heavenly gifts do fall.
Most generous of all, you never deny.
To you, I am grateful, and so mote it be!

Put the candle in a safe, fireproof place, such as a fireplace, and let it burn all night. You will dream of your loved ones, including yourself, receiving a bounty of material and spiritual wealth.

POT of GOLD: AN ABUNDANCE BLESSING

Cauldron magic is more about the act of brewing something new than it is about purification by water. To attract money, fill a big pot with fresh water and place it on your altar during the waxing moon.

Pour into it an offering of a cup of milk mixed with honey. Toss handfuls of dried chamomile, woodruff, moss, and vervain into the cauldron.

With your head raised, say aloud:

I call upon you, gods and goddesses of old, to fill my purse with gold. In return, I offer you honey's gold and mother's milk. With harm to none and blessings to thee, I honor you for bringing me health and prosperity.

TURN, TURN, TURN: TO EVERYTHING THERE IS a SEASONAL ALTAR

There are many reasons to create personal altars, and four of those reasons are the seasons of the year. Your altar helps you maintain balance in your life and deepens your spiritual connection to the world around you. A seasonal altar is your tool for ceremonies to honor Mother Nature and connect with the deeper wisdom of the earth.

SPRING

You can create a wonderful outdoor altar for spring by planning two seasons ahead and planting tulip or hyacinth bulbs in a circle. When the flowers begin to bud, place an image

or statue in the center. It could be a
bust of the Greek youth, Hyacinth,
immortalized in myth and in the gor-
geous flower itself.

SUMMER

During this season of sun and heat, the
fullness of life and growth can be cele-
brated with colors of yellow, green, and
red. As you travel on vacation, bring
back shells and stones and create an
altar devoted to this season of joy.

FALL

The leaves are now falling and the harvest is here, calling for a gratitude altar that reflects the bounty and continuance of life. An arrangement of pumpkins, acorns, multicolored branches, and a handsome bouquet of leaves will honor the natural changes that characterize autumn.

WINTER

White and blue represent snow and sky. Star-shaped candles and a bare branch on your altar symbolize this time to go within, explore the inner reaches of self, and draw forth the deepest wisdom for the coming spring.

MAGICAL HERBS

Refer to this list whenever you are setting up your altar and setting your intention for ritual work.

Benzoin can be used for purification, prosperity, work success, mental acuity, and memory.

Camphor can be used for healing, divining the future, curbing excess, especially romantic obsessions, and a surfeit of sexuality.

Cinnamon refreshes and directs spirituality. It is also handy for healing, money, love, lust, personal power, and success with work and creative projects.

Clove is good for bringing money to you, for protection, for your love life, and for helping evade and deter negative energies.

Copal should be used for love and purification.

Frankincense is another spiritual essence that purifies and protects.

Lavender is a plant for happiness, peace, true love, long life, chastity, and is an excellent purifier that aids with sleep.

Myrrh has been considered since ancient times to be deeply sacred. It aids personal spirituality, heals and protects, and can help ward off negative spirits and energies.

Nutmeg is a lucky herb that promotes good health and prosperity and encourages fidelity.

Patchouli stimulates and grounds while engendering both sensuality and encouraging fidelity.

Peppermint is an herb of purification, healing, and love. It supports relaxation and sleep as it helps to increase psychic powers.

Rosemary is good for purification, protection, healing, relaxation, and intelligence. It attracts love and sensuality, helps with memory, and can keep you youthful.

Sage brings wisdom, purification, protection, health, and a long life. It can help make your wishes come true.

Sandalwood is a mystical, healing, protecting essence that helps attract the objects of your hopes and desires and disperses negative energies and spirits.

Star anise is a lucky herb that aids divination and psychism.

Tonka bean brings courage and draws love and money.

Vanilla brings love and enriches your mental capacity.

Wood aloe is good for dressing or anointing talismans and amulets you want to use for protection.

INTENTION CANDLE SPELL

*W*rite your intention on paper and then speak aloud:

Thus I consecrate this candle in the name of [your favorite deity].
So this flame will burn brightly and light my way.

Place the anointed candle in the
candleholder, light it, and say:

Blessed candle, light of the
 Goddess,
I burn this light of [deity's name]*.*
Hear my prayer, O, [name the
 deity]*, hear my need.*
Grant my wish and give me hope.
Do so with all your grace,
And magical speed.

Now read your intention as you wrote it on the paper. Roll the paper into a scroll and, using a few drops of the warm wax from your intention candle, seal your sacred statement. Place the paper on your altar or in a special place where it can be safe until your intention is realized.

RITUAL KNOTTING

*A*ll you need is a paper scroll and a length of red thread or cord. The color red signifies life and active energy. After you feel you have fully focused your energy into the scroll, roll it up.

Now, proceed to tie knots in the order of the following traditional chant:

By knot of one, this ritual is begun.

By knot of two, my wish comes true.

By knot of three, so mote it be.

By knot of four, the magic is even more.

By knot of five, the gods are alive.

By knot of six, my intention is fixed.

*By knot of seven, under the influence
    of heaven.*

By knot of eight, I change my fate.

By knot of nine, all powers are divine.

When you have completed the
knots, tie the cord around your scroll.

INSPIRATION
INFUSIONS

*A*long with healing and energizing properties, herbal teas can aid the mind. Try the following blends:

Bergamot

dissipates negativity and uplifts.

❧

Basil

lends a sense of serenity.

❧

Rosemary

supports physical well-being.

❧

Orange

creates sheer joy.

GETTING GROUNDED THROUGH GUIDED MEDITATION

*B*ecause the world we live in today is very much about getting in your head and staying there, many of us have to make a concentrated effort to become grounded and in touch with our bodies and with the natural world around us.

Grounding is the technique for centering yourself within your being, getting into your body and out of your head. Grounding is the way to reconnect and balance yourself through the power of the element of earth. When you see someone walking past talking on their cell phone, you know that they are not grounded.

WALKING MEDITATION

*A*s you walk, take the time to look and really see what is in your path. For example, my friend Eileen takes a bag with her and picks up every piece of garbage in her path. She does this as an act of love for the earth. During the ten years I have known her, she has probably turned a mountain of garbage into recycled glass, paper, and plastic. Goddess bless!

NEW MOON CANDLE CONSECRATION

If you are looking for love, perform this rite and you will soon find a lover to satisfy your needs. On the night of the next new moon, take two pieces of rose quartz and place them on the floor in the center of your bedroom.

Light two red candles and use this affirming chant:

Beautiful crystal I hold this night,
Flame with love for my delight,
Goddess of Love, I ask of you,
Guide me in the path that is true.
Harm to none as love comes to me.
This I ask and so it shall be.

TWIN HEARTS

Many crystal shops and New Age stores now feature heart-shaped rocks. The next time you see heart-shaped amethyst crystals, buy two right away and give one to your true love. The gift of an amethyst heart will ensure a happy life together and good fortune shared. Sweet!

ROCK YOUR WORLD: STONES FOR SUCCESS

These stones pave the path to prosperity for everyone:

Azurite strengthens mental powers.

Chalcedony gives you get-up-and-go!

Emerald aids in problem solving.

Opal encourages faithful service.

Pearl engenders material wealth.

Quartz helps overcome fear of rejection.

Sapphire helps with goal setting.

Tourmaline promotes an attitude of accomplishment.

ON the RISE WITH ROSE

If you want to jump-start your life and bring about positive change, tap into the power of the rose and red stones. Stones of this color spectrum contain life's energy and can help you become more motivated, energetic, and vibrant. Wear this list of rosy and red stones or

place them on your desk and throughout your home for an instant boost:
alexandrite, carnelian, garnet, red
coral, red jasper, rhyolite, rose jasper,
and ruby.

WONDERFUL WANDS

It is a wonderful thing to make your own wand. Start with a tree branch that has fallen to the ground on its own. Sand and polish the rough edges, as it is a wand and not a weapon. Then give it a good smudging. Hot-glue a large quartz crystal onto the wand near the handle, and hot-glue on any crystals featuring properties that will comple-ment your magic.

MAGIC CORD

This is a rope that binds magic to you and is ideally made from strands of red wool or ribbon. Nine feet long, it is braided and tied into a loop at one end to represent feminine energy and left loose or frayed at the opposing end to signify the complementary male energy. Crystal beads woven onto the strands of the rope can compound its magical quality.

MAGIC ON THE MOVE: PARKING PENDANT

Hang a red jasper crystal attached to a string on your rearview mirror in your car and your parking problems will soon be over.

When you need a spot, touch the jasper and say, "See the parking spot; be the parking spot." Remember to always give thanks to the parking gods and goddesses to remain in their favor.

SPACE INVADERS

Do you have nosy neighbors or a nightmare roommate? Combat other people's cluelessness with crystals! If you have problems with the people next door, place jet at your door or bury it by the fence. If you have an intrusive housemate or guest, place jet on the mantle or bookshelves and wear jet jewelry to take back your personal space straightaway.

MOONSTONE MIRROR MAGIC

Moonstone is a psychic mirror, especially for females. Wise women of ancient India were the first to figure this out. If you are feeling out-of-sorts or off-center, turn to this lovely stone, sacred to the shining orb in our night sky. Under moonlight, gaze first at the moon and then at your smooth, round moonstone and look for the answer to your personal mystery. A message will come to you in the form of a dream this night. Keep a journal at your bedside to record this moonlit message.

BLISSFUL
BED BLESSING

*A*noint your bed with this special charm. In a red cup, mix a half-teaspoon of jasmine oil and a half-teaspoon of rose oil. Take a cotton ball and dip it into the bliss oil. Touch it to your clean sheets seven times from where you rest your head to the feet, for each chakra point.

Then speak aloud:

In this bed, I show my love.
In this bed, I share my body.
In this bed, I give my heart.
In this bed, we are as one.
Here, my happiness lies as I give
and live in total joy.
Blessed be to me and thee.

Now, lie down and roll around in
the bed. After all, that is what it is for!

ORAL FIXATION: MAGICAL MEALS

I highly recommend consuming these aphrodisiacs for your pleasure:

Almonds or erotically shaped marzipan.

Arugula, also called "rocket seed." Need I say more?

Avocado, referred to by the ancient Aztecs as the "testicle tree."

Bananas and banana flowers, which have phallic shapes.

Chocolate, quite rightly called "the food of the Gods."

Honey, as the term "honeymoon" came from a bee-sweetened drink served to newlyweds.

ECSTATIC ELIXIR

*E*lixirs are very simple potions made by placing a crystal or gemstone in a glass of water for at least seven hours. Remove the stone and drink the crystallized water. The water will now carry the vibrational energy of the stone, the very essence of the crystal.

Place into a glass of water:

Carnelian · Garnet · Rough ruby ·
Red coral · Red jade · Jasper ·
Red sardonyx · Cuprite
Aventurine · Red calcite

Mix and match and remember, if
you only have access to a rough ruby
and a tiny chunk of jasper, so be it—
that is still a lot of love in a jar!

Place the elixir in the love corner of
your room or on your altar. Light

amber incense and a red candle and
speak aloud:

This jade is my joy, the garnet of my
grace.

Leave the water on your altar for
seven hours or overnight and drink it
upon awakening. Your life energy will
quicken and you should feel very
upbeat and good to go.

BELTANE TWIST

*B*eltane is the sexiest high holiday for witches, and it is anticipated all year. Witchy ones celebrate Beltane on the very last eve of April, and it is traditional for the festivities to go on all night. This is a holiday for feasting, dancing, laughter, and lots of lovemaking. May Day, when the sun returns, is when

revelers erect a beribboned maypole
and dance around in gay garb followed by pagan picnicking and
sensory siestas.

BELTANE BREW

*H*oneyed mead is revered as the drink of choice for this red hot holy day. It is an aphrodisiac, and with its sticky sweetness, it is perfect for dribbling on your lover's body, only to be licked off. This is my special recipe for honeyed mead, handed down through generations of Celtic witches.

Combine:

One quart honey

Three quarts distilled water

Mix the honey and water and boil
for five minutes. You can vary the
herbs to your liking, but I prefer a
teaspoon each of clove, nutmeg,
cinnamon, and allspice. Add a packet
of yeast and mix. Put in a large container. Cover with plastic wrap and
allow it to rise and expand. Store the
mixture in a dark place and let it sit
for seven days.

Then, refrigerate for three days while the sediment settles at the bottom. Strain and store in a colored glass bottle, preferably green, in a cool, dark place. You can now drink it, but it is even tastier after it has aged for a period of at least seven months. This Beltane Brew packs a punch—it's 60 proof!

FESTIVE FRIDAY FROLIC

*V*enus rules this most popular day of the week. Small wonder this is the night for a tryst. To prepare yourself for a night of lovemaking, you should take a Goddess bath with the following potion in a special cup or bowl. I call mine the Venus Vial.

Combine:

   One cup sesame oil
   Six drops orange blossom oil
   Four drops gardenia oil

Stir with your fingers six times,
silently repeating three times:

I am daughter of Venus, I embody
   love.
My body is a temple of pleasure,
And I am all that is beautiful.
   Tonight,

I will drink fully from the cup of love.

Pour the Venusian mixture into a steaming bath and meditate on your evening plans. As you rise from your bath, repeat the Venus spell once more.

Don't use a towel, but allow yourself to dry naturally. Your lover will compliment the softness of your skin, and indeed, you will be at your sexiest. The rest is up to you.

TIME IS
ON YOUR SIDE

A gift of a clock is lucky.
Luckier still is to hear two
clocks chiming together at a happy
moment. If you are kissing, happy in
company, meeting someone you like,
concluding a business deal or launch-
ing a project, or indeed, in the midst

of any other hopeful occasion, and you hear two clocks striking together, link fingers with the other person, or kiss them on the cheek.

Say: "Two clocks have struck, / 'Tis set for luck." Take careful note of the hour.

For the next two days, observe the hour again and think of the event that has just taken place; wish hard for luck on that matter once again.

Good luck will surely attend you—
whatever the matter on hand con-
cerns.

BLUEBIRDS of HAPPINESS CHARMS

*B*luebirds are so famous they have given their name to the bluebird of happiness. The robin has been associated with the same signs of cheerfulness and joy. Seeing a bluebird or robin, you should immediately make a wish: it must be something unselfish, and not dependent on any-one else.

As the bird flies off, set your wish ascending. Wish hard for steadily increasing happiness and release from strains. Whether a bluebird or a robin, if you see the bird again with a few days in exactly the same place, your wish will certainly be granted.

Here are some more magical wings and prayers:

Crow feathers: These indicate loss and mourning. Try not to be frightened but look at them as indicators of the cycles of life, death, and rebirth.

Hummingbird feathers: These bring joy, beauty, and bliss. Take time out to have a good time and to share with the people you love.

Swan feathers: These are the sign of grace. As swans mate for life, a swan feather can also mean a soul mate or good relationship is on the horizon.

Yellowhammer feathers: These are the symbol for hearth and home. Seeing a yellowhammer feather in your path means you will have a happy new home.

Magpie feathers: These are just plain good medicine for any kind of illness. Magpies bring purification.

HAPPINESS WITH A BOTTLE SPELL

This does not have to be a champagne cork—they are all lucky. When a bottle is shared and the occasion is a happy event or joyous moment, secret away the cork from the bottle, making a wish for repetition of the pleasure as you do so, and placing a coin in a slit in the top of the cork.

Now you must sleep on the cork every night (under your pillow) and keep it in your pocket all the next day. Rub the cork any day thereafter when you wish to hear from the other person or people who shared the bottle with you; do not wish for love but rather for continuing happiness. The cork symbolizes buoyancy, not love.

Celebrate these events throughout the year to find your lucky cork:

January 1: New Year's Day

February 14: St. Valentine's Day

March 8: International Women's Day

April 22: Earth Day

May 1: May Day, Baltane

June 19: Juneteenth

July 20: National Moon Day

August 4: Dom Perignon invents champagne in 1693—celebrate!

September 20: International Day of Peace

October 15: Festival of Mars (Ancient Rome)

November 5: Guy Fawkes Day

December 5: International Volunteers Day

SYLVIAN SPELL

This is a lovely spell to do if you are given a small tree as a gift, to wish for strength and good health for you and your love. Before you plant the sapling, tie a bow in some colored ribbon, and plant the bow with a small heart symbol in the soil under the roots of the tree.

After you have planted the tree,

water it well—especially with one or two tears of love, if possible! Make a wish that both you and your love will grow strong and enduring as the tree takes root and begins to flourish.

When the tree bears its first leaf, press it in a book associated with the one you love. As long as you tend your tree with love, you will both enjoy blooming health and vitality.

SACRED SAFFRON SPELL

*S*affron water is made by boiling one teaspoon of saffron in two cups of distilled water. Dip your hands in the water, touch your "third eye" at the center of your forehead and speak aloud:

Ishtar, Isis, Astarte—fill me with
  your presence.
This night, I am whole. I am at
  peace.
With each breath, you do inspire.
So mote it be.

CLARITY INFUSION

I recommend growing a pot of hardy sage so you can always clear energy and increase your psychic potential. Another useful herb is mint, which comes from the Latin *mentha*, and literally means "thought." It is called the flower of eternal refreshment. Woven into a crown, it bestows brilliance, artistic inspiration, and prophetic ability. Burned, it is especially potent.

Here is a wonderfully simple tool for awakening the mind and attuning to the high powers. Take dried mint stalks and dried sage in equal parts and roll together into a wand. Bind with multi-colored string, and before any ritual, tarot reading, or spellcrafting, "smudge" your house with the wand by lighting the leafy end and passing the smoke around. This will purify your space.

STEEPED in WISDOM: CUPS of COMFORT

Tea conjures a very powerful alchemy because when you drink it, you take the magic inside. For an ambrosial brew with the power to calm any storm, add a sliver of ginger root and a pinch each of chamomile and peppermint to a cup of hot black tea. Before you drink, pray:

> *This day I pray for calm, for health,*
> *And the wisdom to see the beauty of*
> *each waking moment.*
> *Blessings abound.*
> *So mote it be.*

Herbal teas can also nourish the soul and heal the body:

Blueberry leaf reduces mood swings, evens glucose levels, and helps varicose veins.

Nettle raises the energy level, boosts the immune system, and is packed with iron and vitamins.

Fennel awakens and uplifts, freshens the breath, and aids colon health.

Echinacea lends an increased and consistent sense of well-being, and prevents colds and flu.

Ginger root calms and cheers while aiding digestion, nausea, and circulation.

Dandelion root grounds and centers, provides many minerals and nutrients, and cleanses the liver of toxins.

BLUE MOON
BALM

For a dreary day and a dark mood, use the strength of the ancient unguent myrrh to release both mind and body. This desert plant produces a protective oil, which works as both a sunscreen and a moisturizer. Combine the following oils with either four ounces of unscented body lotion, or two ounces of olive oil or sweet almond oil:

2 drops chamomile oil
2 drops myrrh
8 drops rosemary
8 drops geranium

Shake the oils together and place in a corked pottery jar. Sit quietly in a room lit only by one blue candle, and rub the balm gently into your skin after a bath. Pray aloud:

Work thy spell to heal and nurse.
Blessed balm, banish my pain.
Harm to none and health to all.

INSPIRATION INFUSION

Teas brewed from a single herb are commonly called "simples." I love that phrase of olden times. Experience has taught me that these simples often have the most intensity, since the very singleness of the herb gives it potency.

A simple made from one of the following herbs enhances mental clarity, even clairvoyance. This will jumpstart you on your path toward any creative pursuit. Here is a recipe for a very inspired tea:

Boil one pint of spring water. Place into your favorite crockery teapot a half-ounce of any ONE of the following herbs: rosemary, mugwort, yarrow, or thyme.

Steep for ten minutes and strain with a nonmetallic strainer, like cheesecloth or an inexpensive bamboo strainer. Sweeten with a little honey; I recommend clover honey because you get the added benefits of clover's lucky powers. Sip this brew while relaxing, and be inspired!

SYMBOL WRITING

If you wish to make direct contact with your unconsciousness, here is a way to see through the veil between two worlds and enter the recesses of your mind. At any herbal store or metaphysical shop, obtain dried mugwort, dried patchouli, or wormwood. The latter is a bit harder to come by, but worth the try.

Crumble any one of these herbs between your hands until it is gently ground into an almost powdery consistency. Pour the herb into a baking pan. Make sure the crumbled herb dust is evenly spread over the surface of the pan.

Light yellow candles and close your eyes. Take the forefinger of your left hand and touch the center of the pan. Run your finger back and forth in a completely random pattern—don't think, just rely on your instincts for

two minutes. Open your eyes, look at
the pattern you have drawn, and write
down what the symbols and designs
bring to mind. Also write down the
thoughts you were having while you
were drawing.

SEEDS *of* CHANGE

Nature is the ultimate creator, and by making this grow you will tap directly into this life force. Get an array of seed packets and start a magic garden that will help you to sow fertile new projects and get them off the ground, so to speak.

On a New Moon day, draw a square in your yard or planter with a willow stick, oak stick, or wand and mark each corner with a candle—

one **orange** for higher intelligence,
one **green** for creativity and growth,
one **blue** for serenity and goodness,
and one **white** for purification.

Repeat this chant as you light each candle:

*Mother Gaia, I turn to you to help
  me to renew,
Under this New Moon and in this
  old Earth.
Blessed be.*

Poke the seeds under the soil with
your fingers and tamp them down
with your wand. Gently water your
new moon garden and start a new
project the very next day.

SANCTUARY SPELL

To anoint your home a sacred space and protect you from harm, rub any one of the following essential oils, undiluted, on your doorjamb:

Cinnamon · Clover · Cypress

Dragon's blood · Frankincense

Walk through the door and close it securely. Take the remaining essential oil and anoint every other door and window. At the witching hour, midnight, light anointed white candles and place them in every doorway and windowsill, and sing:

My home is my temple, and here I will live and love and be healed. And so it is by magic sealed.

ENCOURAGEMENT INFUSION

*O*n a Sunday, or any day you need encouragement, set aside a half-hour of quiet time and brew up some willpower to help you in any creative endeavor. Light a white candle anointed with peppermint oil and light spicy incense (cinnamon works well, if you can get it).

Take a sprig of mint, warm milk, and cinnamon sticks and stir together clockwise in a white mug. Say aloud:

Herb of minthe and spicy mead,
Today is the day I shall succeed
In every word and every deed.

Quaff the cup and "sit for a spell," eyes closed, envisioning your new horizons. Keep the cinnamon sticks on your altar as a symbol of the power of encouraging words.

ENCHANTED EYES

If you are an artist of any sort, you most likely use your eyes to create, so caring for them is essential. Take two small muslin bags and three ounces of dried chamomile flowers. Divide the herb in half, stuff the bags, and sew them shut.

Place the eye bags in a bowl and pour a quarter cup of boiling water over them. Cover them and let sit for a half-hour. Squeeze the excess water out of the bags and place over your eyes. Your eyes and your artistic vision should both be rejuvenated quickly.

THE BURNING BOWL

*H*ere is a wonderful way friends can help each other get rid of fears, creative blocks, and the shrill voice of the inner critic. Ideally, this spell is done during the waning moon or on November 1st or December 31st—the witchy holidays when the veil between worlds is believed to be thinnest.

Get a metal kettle and an outdoor firepot or little grill, and for each of the friends you have invited, a pen and two pieces of paper. Sit around the fire, relax, and talk about what challenges you face in attaining your artistic goals.

Write on a piece of paper what comes up for you. Go around the circle and read from your list of blocks. Then, with great intention, place each paper on the fire. After everyone is done, silently meditate, and write your hope for the future. Now, reversing the order of speaking, go around the circle and share your dreams. Fold the paper and carry it with you in your purse or wallet. Your vision for the future will take on a life of its own.

DIS-SPELLING
FEAR

For overcoming stage fright or to psych yourself up before a performance, opening, or speaking engagement, you can turn to your banishing block touchstone.
Sit on the floor, legs crossed, and breathe deeply nine times. Take the

touchstone into your hands and
chant:

> *That which came from the sky,*
> *   enter into me.*
>
> *As was the moon full, so am I now.*
>
> *And so I go, with this light, full and*
> *   bright.*
>
> *So mote it be.*

  Repeat this at least six times, until
you feel the energy of the stone passing into you. Now, go conquer!

BLESSING MEDITATION

*S*it in a comfortable position in front of your serenity altar and meditate. Think about your blessings. What are you grateful for at this moment? There is a powerful magic in recognizing all that you possess. Breathe steadily and deeply, inhaling and exhaling slowly for twenty minutes. Then chant:

*Great Goddess, giver of all the fruits of
  this earth,*

Of all bounty, beauty, and well-being,

*Bless all who give and receive these
  gifts.*

*I am made of sacred earth, purest
  water, sacred fire, and wildest wind.*

Blessing upon me. Blessing upon thee,

Mother Earth and Sister Sky.

So mote it be.

VENUS SKIN-PRESERVING POTION

You will notice that many witches appear ageless. There is a good reason for this: We take good care of our skin and heighten the health of our complexions with a Venusian prescription for eternal youth. Combine these oils:

2 ounces sweet almond
2 drops clary sage
2 drops chamomile
2 drops myrrh
2 drops rosemary
2 drops geranium

Before you anoint your skin each
night, utter this spell:

Goddess of Love, Goddess of
Light—hear this prayer.
Your youth and beauty eternal
please share.
So mote it be.

Rub the potion on your face and rinse off for healthy skin and a radiant glow.

DREAM MIST POTION

*S*leeping on crisp, clean, herb-scented sheets always make for the soundest sleep and delicious dreams. Here is a potion for dreamers:

4 drops lavender oil

3 drops chamomile oil
3 drops orange oil
4 ounces distilled spring water

Shake the oils and water in a colored-glass spray bottle or mister. Fifteen minutes before you retire, spray your bed linens, bath towel, pillow, and all around your room. You may want to keep a dream journal by your bed to record what happens during the night.

CAKES and ALE

Here is a pagan ritual I have performed on weekends, calling it Saturn Day Night Fever. Over the years, I have added many embellishments, such as astrological or holiday themes. The basic ritual, Cakes and Ale, however, is a timeless and powerful classic.

Gather a group of friends either outdoors under the moon or in a room large enough for dancing, drumming, and singing. Have the guests bring a cake of their choice as well as a cider, mead, beer, or juice to share. Place the offerings in the center, on an altar table. Then light a sage leaf and green and brown candles for home and hearth.

Once everyone is seated, the host or designated leader intones:

Gods of Nature, bless these cakes,
That we may never suffer hunger.
Goddess of the Harvest, bless this
ale,
That we may never go without
drink.

The eldest and the youngest of the circle rise and serve the food and drink to everyone in the circle. Last, they serve each other. The ritual leader pronounces the blessing again. Then everyone says together, "Blessed be."

The feasting begins, ideally followed by a lot more ale and lively dancing. A wonderful way to keep a group of friends connected is for a different person to host the circle one Saturday each month.

TRAVEL TALISMANS

Before you travel for work, study, and pleasure, it's good to create charms and talismans of power. You can also craft your own ritual tools from what you gather in your travels. Nature will often provide you with tools: shells, bark, and stones. Pay attention and you will learn much and receive many gifts.

RING of POWER

Most people don't realize that the classic charm bracelet is decorated with magical symbols representing the wearer's wishes. For wealth, wear a Roman coin on your bracelet; for love, try a heart.

For protection, a pure silver ring worn on the right pinkie has the greatest magical power, especially when engraved with your birth sign or astrological glyph and the sacred pentagram. To instill the ring with protective power, clasp it over your heart and call out:

Ring of power, shield and encircle me. Blessed be.

TELEPATHY TEA

The humble dandelion, oft abhorred by lawn keepers, hides its might well. Dandelion root tea can call upon the spirit of anyone whose advice you might need. Simply place the brew on your nightstand and say the spirit's name seven times; he or she will visit your dreams and answer your questions. In Chaucer's day, this method was used to find lost treasures.

PURIFICATION BROOM

A purification broom can be used to purify any space, usually a home space. You can use a home purification broom to clear away bad energy after a fight with a loved one, or if you are feeling blue and want to sweep away bad feelings.

Purchase a broom from a craft fair or broommaker, and add your personal energy to it. You can attach crystals to the handle or wires, or wrap copper wire around the handle. Copper is associated with Venus, and this will lend an aura of beauty as you brush away negativity.

HERBAL HEALING ESSENCE

For an immune system boost, crush a mixture of equal parts rosemary, sandalwood, and the petals of a red carnation. Place the crushed herbs in a colored glass jar filled with virgin olive oil. After seven days' storage on a windowsill so as to be exposed to both Sun and Moon, strain and place the infused oil back into the jar.

You now have a hearty supply of homemade healing oil to use in the bath or to rub on your pulse points: temple, wrists, backs of knees, and behind the ears.

As soon as you feel rundown, one application should make a difference.

PRECIOUS STONES

A charm for solvency is to take seven tiny turquoise stones and put them on your windowsill during a full moon for seven hours. Then pick up the stones and, while holding them in the palm of your hand, speak this wish-spell aloud:

Luck be quick, luck be kind,
And, by lucky seven, good luck will
be mine.
Blessed be.

Carry these lucky stones with you in a bright blue bag and be on the lookout for blessings to shower down upon you. You will probably receive gifts, win free services, and you might literally find money in your path.

OIL of ALLIANCE

*H*ave a girlfriend get-together and mix up a batch of this magical salve:

Lavender is for the east, representing mental clarity and ideas.

Musk is for the south, representing new energies and the winds of change.

Honeysuckle is for the north, representing prosperity and abundance.

Rose is for the west, representing emotions, friendship, and love.

Mix these oils together in equal parts. Then have each friend dip a forefinger into the oil mixture and stir clockwise. Raise the bowl of oil and pray together:

In the name of union,

In the spirit of friendship,
I bless this oil as I exalt the bonds
that bring us together.
And so it shall be.

Complete the consecration by dabbing this magical potion on each other's pulse points: wrists, temples, throat, knees, elbows, over the heart, and behind the ears. Make sure you all leave with your own vial of this potion for future spells that require anointing candles and dabbing pulse points.

CLAIM YOUR SPLENDOR

Throughout your practice, make sure to maintain a sense of personal abundance and acknowledge the great spirit within you. Be grateful for your body and for your health. Stand in front of a mirror, preferably naked, and drop all self-criticism. Concentrate on your real

beauty and envelop yourself with
unconditional self-love. Wrap your
arms around yourself as you say:

> *In Her/His image, I, too, am a*
> *Goddess/God.*
> *I walk in beauty; I am surrounded*
> *by love.*
> *Blessed be.*

Light three candles in your favorite
color and scent. Sit in front of your
altar and meditate on what would

make you achieve your full potential. Do you need to change your health habits? Open your creativity? Concentrate deeply, and choose three wishes. Every night for seven days, repeat this spell:

Today I arise. This night I embrace
My serenity, radiance, splendor,
  and wisdom.
Blessed be.

TAKING THE WATERS

A ritual bath that will simultaneously relax and stimulate you is a rare and wonderful thing. To prepare yourself for a visitation from your preferred muse, take a quart of rough sea salt or Epsom salt and place it in a large bowl. Add the juice from six freshly squeezed lemons and add a half-cup of sesame oil. Stir the mixture until it is moistened thoroughly.

When the tub is one-quarter full, add one-quarter of the salt mixture under the faucet. Breathe in deeply ten times, inhaling and exhaling fully before you recite this:

> *Muse and mistress, I offer myself*
> *to you.*
> *Remove from me any impurities*
> *Of the spirit and mind, I open*

myself to you,

    Both heart and soul.

When the tub is full, step inside and exercise your breath ten more times. Repeat the prayer, and use the rest of the salt to scrub your body. Rest and rejuvenate as long as you like, allowing your imagination to wander freely.

SELF-BLESSING

$\mathcal{T}$he time you take to restore yourself is precious. Perform a self-blessing every day. Take dried sage and aromatic lavender and tie it up in a muslin sack. Breathe in the aroma deeply three times. Beginning at the top of your head, the crown chakra, pass the pouch down to your feet, gently touching your other sacred chakras: throat, solar plexus,

stomach, and pelvis. Then, holding
the bag of herbs over your heart,
speak aloud:

Gone are the sorrows, illness, and
  woe,
Here wisdom and health begin to
  flow.
My heart is whole, joy fills my soul.
Blessed be me.

VISION INCENSE

*A*nytime you want to fill your space with an inspirational aroma, burn this incense for heightened senses. On a Wednesday, use a mortar and pestle to grind and mix the following dried herbs:

One part clove
Three parts chicory root
Three parts cinquefoil

Burn the herbs in a fireproof piece of pottery or glass bowl. If the new moon falls on this particular Wednesday, so much the better—the incense will be even more powerful.

MOOD MAGIC SPRAY

To sweeten a sour mood, this recipe works wonders on you or anyone in your environment who might need a lift. Combine the following essential oils:

Two drops of peppermint
Two drops of bergamot
Two drops of lavender

Four drops of rosemary
Four drops of tea tree

Add the mixture to a quart of distilled water and spray the air while
chanting:

Gloom and doom be gone.
Welcome, sweet spirits, into this
*   house.*
Whit harm to none.
So mote it be.

SPIRITUAL SPRING CLEANING: THE BEAN BLESSING

*N*ew seasons bring about the need for new energies. Here is an ancient way of casting out "the old"

and bringing new tidings and positive
new change for your friendships and
family. Buy a big bag of dried beans
and invite all your friends over. In
ancient times, many pagan people—
from the Greeks to the Incan Indi-
ans—believed that beans contained
evil spirits.

Go to your roof or wherever you
can "get high." Give everyone a handful of beans and start throwing them
down one at a time, with each toss
calling out whatever you want to kiss

goodbye—a job, a bad relationship, bad habits, whatever your personal demons may be.

After you have discarded all the discord from your life, you and your friends can celebrate your life and your clean new slate.

Cerridwen Greenleaf is a poet and medieval scholar, practicing witch, and astrologer. She leads Wicca workshops and retreats throughout the U.S, and has published a number of books on witchcraft.

This book has been bound using
handcraft methods and Smyth-
sewn to ensure durability.

Designed by Amanda Richmond.

Edited by Zachary Leibman.

The text was set in
Lomba and LaPortentia.